18 Sangrias

María M. Cuevas Lou

BookLeaf Publishing

Presentation by *BookLeaf Publishing*

Web: www.bookleafpub.com

E-mail: info@bookleafpub.com

ISBN: 9789395756471

First edition 2022

DEDICATION

To my father, that inspired me to write and love the art of literature.

And to my mother, who always supported me with my dreams.

ACKNOWLEDGEMENT

Thank you to the people that came into my life that gifted me some of the experiences. And thank you to one special person that has always pushed me to make my dreams come true. Has always pushed me out of my comfort zone and helped me with this project.

PREFACE

Some of these poems are based on personal experiences. Others have been based on fiction which had lead to accumulate twenty one of these poems. The dynamic of having a drink with the people being described in the poems, has made this an interesting point of view experience. I invite you to go through these drinks with me and get to know their drinkers.

Apple-Kneel

He shows confidence while walking
Is timid and careful with his words
After half of his drink he is already comfortable

His dirty blonde hair
And his firm hands
I can see the mystery in his eyes

I like that after his drink is done
He becomes amorous

I like the confidence that is shown with time
And the mystery that is being provoked through
a smile

Bourbon

Direct and dry with his words
He is the bare description of his drink

He seems arrogant and charming
But the more I stare into his blue eyes
The more I lean into giving him the second drink

Being composed is something difficult to do in
his presence
He knows he irradiates such a confident vibe
He grabs my hand and I take no offense

Churchill

Smooth fare skin and a warm hug is what I
receive
This one is hard to decipher

Confident but cautious
We share the same interests for the arts
The strong smell of his drink makes me
nauseous
With his charms he plays his cards

He is inviting to have a good time
Even though he hides his sad emotions through
nice ones
It's intriguing the idea of having another drink

Daiquiri

Arms covered in tattoos
Silver chunky rings around all fingers except his
left ring finger
Big silver and thread made bracelets accompany
his writs

His style shows freedom and power
His sunglasses controlling our surroundings
He grabs my hand and is gentle

We share a passion for music and cinema
Ballads of high pitch notes
Classic movies with multicultural celebrities

He is soft and sweet
Quiet but interested in what I have to say
His charming behavior overpowers his tough
look
He whispers a wish
Of staying like this forever

El Presidente

You want his attention because he's that type of
person
That makes you feel good when he stares at you

He is cold at the beginning with his words
Not showing interest at all
Moving his cocktail glass while staring at the
candle light
Questioning why he is here

Eyes inviting me to the prohibited
It sounds like a fun experience and adventure

Half a drink down and now he's more forward
than ever
Pressing his lips twice on my hand
I bite in

But now he is done with the chase
He won my attention
And now I can't see his face

French 75

A hand on my back gives chills down my spine
This one is perfect
The smile
The emerald green eyes
And a soothing voice

When I hear my name with his accent
Not only sounds elegant
A fresh scent
He speaks humble about himself
But he is intelligent

I could give him the drink
But I want to be chased by him
He wants more of me
He is eloquent

Gin Fizz

A façade of having many around
Instead he craves for alone time
Just looking for a mind to connect with

He thinks he'll drown
His aura in grime
And there's a myth

Only one person can save him from his misery
The opportunity in rescissory
No one is good enough to stop the pain
I want to help
I want to stop the pain
And give the drink away

Embrace him and show him what he could be
If he'd let life give him glee

Harvey Wallbanger

One wrong move and I know I'll get hurt
And old flame that once was ours
If remorse could take a human form
I'd be sitting in front of it

You never stop loving them
Because they're fresh like oranges
And sweet like cherries

They feel like you have betrayed them
It is over
I know he could hurt me

But I still ache for him
To embrace his warmth
And feel like I'm heard

Jack and Coke

A simple drink
Like a simple man
He's sweet when he greets me

Opens the door and lets me by
Holds the seat for me
Takes my coat and places it on the chair

A gentleman indeed
Yet simple

He is timid but listens when I talk
Intrigued in my stories
Showing how passionate he is with his career

Simple but sweet
Simple but cares
Simple but a gentleman
And I want that second drink but I don't give in

Kir Royal

This man is the one we all see in the movies
Arrogant and rude
With charms on his looks

One minute you despise him and you wish to
leave
He smiles
He flirts
He compliments me
And then I fall for it

But now he shows he cares for me
Maybe I'm wrong with his impression
He has soft brown eyes
Soft caramel hair

The waiter slips my drink on my dress and he
transforms
He is upset and tells him off
He's sweet and careful now

Helps me with my dress
And gives me his coat to cover from the mess
It's hard not to ask for a second drink

Lime Rickey

I suck in a huge breath
I shake my head
I give him a quick kiss on the cheek

An old love
And you'd wonder why is back

Was it the memories we shared
The goals we had
The comfort found in each other?

Is it now the right time?
Would we leave our differences on a side to be
together?

I miss the hot coco and snowy nights
The holding hands underneath the stars
Golden afternoons with the waves touching our
feet
Only time could tell if this is for me

Martini

Ah yes
Typical playboy with a right shirt
Nice smile and bright golden eyes

Compliments float around us
Drinks are almost done and I want more
He is what he drinks

Bold and risky
Glamorous and trendy
Known but not everyone can enjoy it

Promises of traveling the world are made
Is the material interest that is there
But to think about a good time he can give

Nixon

He is the combination of a risk and madness
The adrenaline runs through his veins
Excitement can be seen through him

He calls himself a heathen and an anarchist
Loves to feel the power in his hands
And wants to name me his queen in battle
The use is tempting

Two people crazy enough to love each other that
same night?
The admiration and adoration he'd give me
I want to taste the power on my fingertips
I could rule with him

Only to think I would need another drink
Is he worth it?
Would he betray me after the power is gained?
I want the risk
But I hesitate to give in

Ouzini

Ginger hair and golden freckles
Yellow aura
Like a gentle sunshine

His story covering his arms in colorful tattoos
He looks like a normal guy
But he is full of happiness
We share the same passion for music

A soft ballad plays
And the night is gentle to us
Hopeless romantic
He invites me for a dance

His touch is warm
And half of the drink is gone
He wraps around his arm
And now our bodies unite as one

We speak through our eyes
The tension is there
The drink is gone
And I have no air

Pisco Sour

Raw and sweet
Just like his drink
Sitting across me

With one look
Everything goes quiet
Words are delicate and direct
Provoking chills down my spine

He speaks about home
But sounds like he's out of this world
He shows compassion for his mother
But resentment for his father

Mischievous promises
Big dreams
And I'm all in it
One sip of his drink
And his spirit lifts

There's no sexual connection
But interest in our souls
Great minds sharing the moment
And now we have mutual goals

Half of his drink is gone
But he takes his time
He knows I won't say yes right away
He knows this is not done
He wants to commit a crime
Of freezing the day

Now the glasses are empty
And he knows I'm for the chase
He promises he'll be back
To steal me away

Rum

An interesting look
Smell of the ocean breeze
He sounds like someone out of a book
Everything about him is a tease

Speaks of adventures
But is not stable
Wants to travel and not settle
And I don't know if I'm able

I want his free life
And he wants me to come alongside
I politely decline
But that second drink is in my mind

Sidecar

Fair skin and cold hands with a drink in hand
Has mentioned he is not worth it
But he is willing to try
I understand
He's handsome, I admit

He knows what he wants
Not afraid to take risks to protect me
He says he hunts
And wants to set me free

His drink is gone
He stands up
And says he'll be back
To take me home

Tequila

If the sea could travel across I'd say I'm looking
right at it
These eyes are blue as the ocean
Pure and shinny

But the hair
Dark like ashes
Smooth like silk

I like the way his smile curves up on a side
Showing a sweet dimple
While he talks about the sky

He talks about the stars
And how he wants to go to Mars
Even though his drink is dry
He keeps the conversation alive

The drink is small and leaves no room to talk
I want to know more about those blue eyes
And why they tend to look so sad

There's a past and I want to know why
He hurts so bad
And hides it behind a mask